180 ESSENTIAL VOCABULARY WORDS FOR 6TH GRADE

Independent Learning Packets That Help
Students Learn the Most Important Words
They Need to Succeed in School

Linda Ward Beech

NEW YORK • TORONTO • LONDON • AUCKLAND • SYDNEY
MEXICO CITY • NEW DELHI • HONG KONG • BUENOS AIRES

Teaching *Resources*

Editor: Mela Ottaiano
Cover design: Brian LaRossa
Interior design: Melinda Belter
Interior illustrations: Mike Moran

ISBN-13: 978-0-439-89737-2
ISBN-10: 0-439-89737-8

1 2 3 4 5 6 7 8 9 10   40   15 14 13 12 11 10 09

TABLE OF CONTENTS

Introduction

Academic vocabulary refers to words that are commonly found in textbooks and used in assignments, content area standards, and standardized tests. Just as specialized words are used in fields such as journalism, medicine, and law enforcement, academic vocabulary is the language of the classroom, school, and the educational process. Recognizing these words and comprehending what they mean is, therefore, crucial to a student's academic success. The purpose of this book is to help students become familiar with the academic vocabulary most often used at their grade level. In this way, they will be better prepared to understand and successfully complete classroom work, homework assignments, and tests.

The lessons in this book are organized around curriculum areas and other common school topics. Each four-page lesson introduces ten words and provides various ways for students to explore their meaning and usage. The lessons are intended as independent activities with some teacher support.

Materials

As you introduce the lessons, be sure to have the following items available:

Dictionaries
Thesauruses
Writing tools or computers
Student portfolios of written work

Tips for Using the Lessons

• Make a practice of using the lesson words often in classroom discussions and assignments. Call attention to these words as they come up.

• Consider having students make a set of word cards for each lesson. You might also make a class set and place it in your language arts center.

• Many words have more than one meaning, including some that are not given in the lesson. Point out additional meanings or invite students to discover and share them.

• Review parts of speech with students before each lesson. Many words can be used as more than one part of speech, including examples that are not given in this book. Encourage students to monitor their use of these words.

• Be sure to have students complete the Portfolio Page assignments on the second page of each lesson. Add your own writing assignments as well. Applying the lesson words in independent writing activities is essential in making the words part of students' vocabulary.

• Encourage students to consult more than one reference and to compare information.

 **TEXT MESSAGE** You'll find a complete alphabetized list of all the lesson words in the Word List at the back of the book. Each page number listed identifies the first page of the lesson in which the word is found.

Lesson Organization

Each lesson is four pages long and introduces ten academic words.

The first lesson page includes:

lesson words

statement of lesson focus

simple sentences explaining meaning of words

cloze exercise *

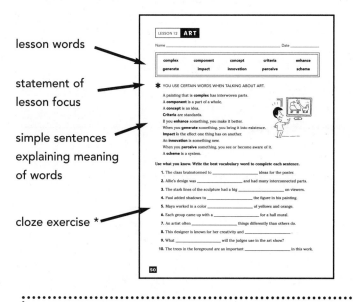

The second page includes:

lesson words

one or more exercises focusing on meaning

Portfolio Page writing assignment

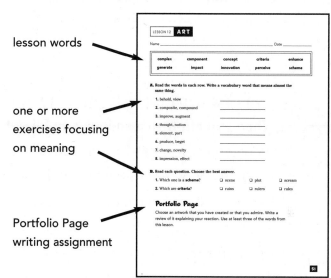

> * ALERT STUDENTS TO LOOK AT THE SUBJECTS OF THE CLOZE SENTENCES to determine if they are singular or plural because that will affect the form of the verbs they use. Students should also use the correct verb tense in these sentences. For nouns, students should determine whether they need to use the singular or plural form.

The third page includes:

lesson words

two or three exercises focusing on suffixes, prefixes, other meanings, parts of speech, word roots, or word structure

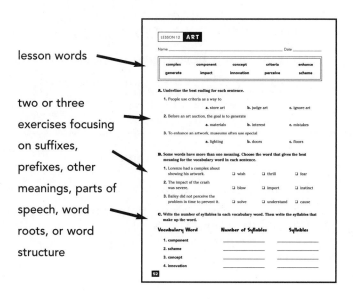

The fourth page includes:

a puzzle, game, maze, or other learning activity using the words

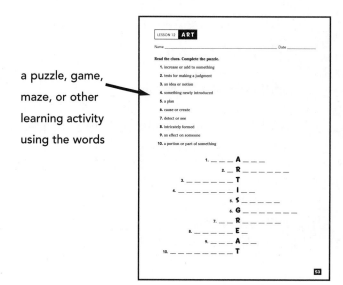

SCHOOL

Name _____ Date _____

| accomplish | application | consult | enrich | exercise |
| foundation | institution | interact | maximize | motivation |

✴ SOME WORDS ARE USEFUL TO KNOW BECAUSE THEY RELATE TO SCHOOL.

If you **accomplish** a task, you carry it out.

When you apply to a school, you fill out an **application**.

When you **consult** a teacher, you ask for advice.

Reading good literature will **enrich**, or add to, your understanding of human nature.

Learning about **exercise** or fitness is part of your education.

A **foundation** is the base, or basis, on which something rests.

An **institution** is an organization, such as a school.

Things that **interact** act upon, or with, each other.

Try to **maximize**, or make the most of, your time at school.

Motivation is an incentive for doing something.

Use what you know. Write the best vocabulary word to complete each sentence.

1. Jared wrote quickly to _____ the time allowed for the test.

2. Minna decided to _____ Mr. Ellis about her project.

3. How will the teams _____ with each other at the pre-game party?

4. Hannah ran laps on the track to get _____ each day.

5. This school is an important _____ in the community.

6. Mr. Toro had a lot to _____ before class began.

7. Dexter has the _____ to do well in school this year.

8. Students who want to work on the school paper must complete an

_____ for a position.

9. Art and music classes can _____ a student's life.

10. Respect is one _____ of a good friendship.

SCHOOL

Name _____ Date _____

| accomplish | application | consult | enrich | exercise |
| foundation | institution | interact | maximize | motivation |

A. Write a vocabulary word that is a synonym for each underlined word or phrase in the sentences.

1. The hopeful student filled out a <u>form</u> for the job. _____

2. The captain <u>conferred with</u> the coach before the game. _____

3. Careful research is the <u>backbone</u> of a good report. _____

4. The teacher and students <u>relate</u> well with each other. _____

B. Read the first word in each row. Circle a word in the row that is a synonym and underline a word that is an antonym.

1. **enrich**	enroll	excite	improve	diminish
2. **motivation**	inspiration	movement	assistance	disincentive
3. **accomplish**	fail	achieve	accommodate	gather
4. **maximize**	captivate	increase	minimize	monitor
5. **institution**	entrance	individual	instinct	organization
6. **exercise**	exertion	crush	inactivity	exhaust

Portfolio Page

Find or take a picture of your school, then write a paragraph about it.
Use at least three vocabulary words from this lesson.

Name _____ Date _____

| accomplish | application | consult | enrich | exercise |
| foundation | institution | interact | maximize | motivation |

A. Write a vocabulary word that is related to each word below. Then write another word that is related to both words. Use related words you already know or find words in a resource.

Word	Related Vocabulary Word	Another Related Word
1. apply	_____	_____
2. act	_____	_____
3. motivate	_____	_____
4. institute	_____	_____
5. founder	_____	_____

B. Write a sentence to answer each question.

1. What do you hope to **accomplish** in school this year?

_____

2. What subjects help to **enrich** your life?

_____

3. What is your favorite form of **exercise**?

_____

4. How do you plan to **maximize** your talents?

_____

5. Why is it helpful to **consult** with someone before making a big decision?

_____

180 Essential Vocabulary Words for 6th Grade © 2009 by Linda Ward Beech, Scholastic Teaching Resources

Name _____ Date _____

Read the clues. Complete the puzzle using vocabulary words.

1. a college is an example of one

2. a way of staying fit

3. bring about

4. inducement

5. request for admittance

6. talk over

7. groundwork

8. connect with

9. make more meaningful

10. enhance

1. __ __ **S** __ __ __ __ __ __ __

2. __ __ __ __ **C** __ __ __

3. __ __ __ __ __ __ __ __ __ **H**

4. __ **O** __ __ __ __ __ __ __

5. __ __ __ __ __ __ __ __ __ __ **O** __

6. __ __ __ __ __ **L** __

7. __ __ __ __ **D** __ __ __

8. __ __ __ __ __ **A** __ __

9. __ __ __ __ __ __ **Z** __

10. **E** __ __ __ __ __

Name _____ Date _____

annotate	characteristic	derive	irony	literal
reaction	significance	stress	symbolize	version

✴ YOU USE CERTAIN WORDS WHEN YOU TALK ABOUT LITERATURE.

If you **annotate** a work of literature, you include notes.

A **characteristic** is a feature.

Derive means "to come from a certain source."

Irony is a literary device in which words suggest the opposite of their meaning for humorous purposes.

A **literal** meaning reflects exactly what a word means.

A **reaction** is an action or attitude aroused by something.

Significance means "importance."

To **stress** is to accent.

Symbolize means to "serve as a symbol."

A **version** is an account of something.

Use what you know. Write the best vocabulary word to complete each sentence.

1. Kara had a strong _____ to this book.

2. This story _____ from a Greek myth.

3. What is the _____ of this passage from Hamlet's speech?

4. In this speech, the playwright uses _____ to show the character's scorn.

5. There are many _____ of the Cinderella story.

6. Long sentences are a _____ of that author's work.

7. The poet uses the moon to _____ loneliness in this poem.

8. The editor of the book has _____ the stories to help the reader.

9. When you pronounce a word, you _____ certain syllables.

10. Poets often use a figurative instead of _____ meaning of a word.

180 Essential Vocabulary Words for 6th Grade © 2009 by Linda Ward Beech, Scholastic Teaching Resources

Name _____ Date _____

annotate	characteristic	derive	irony	literal
reaction	significance	stress	symbolize	version

A. Read the words in each row. Write a vocabulary word that means the same or almost the same thing.

1. emphasize, accentuate _____

2. signify, represent _____

3. translation, explanation _____

4. come from, trace _____

5. importance, meaning _____

6. trait, quality _____

7. faithful, exact _____

B. Read each question. Choose the best answer.

1. Which one is a **reaction**? ❏ survey ❏ surplus ❏ surprise

2. Why do you **annotate**? ❏ continue ❏ comment ❏ accelerate

3. Which one is **irony**? ❏ wit ❏ wig ❏ whim

Portfolio Page

Write a paragraph giving your reaction to a book you have read. Use at least three vocabulary words from this lesson.

Name _____ Date _____

annotate	characteristic	derive	irony	literal
reaction	significance	stress	symbolize	version

A. The lesson words below have suffixes. A suffix is added to the end of a word to change its meaning and often its part of speech. Underline the suffix in each word. Then, write a sentence using the word. Use a dictionary if needed.

1. ironical _____

_____

2. stressful _____

_____

3. annotation _____

_____

4. characteristically _____

_____

5. reactionary _____

_____

B. Write a vocabulary word that is an antonym of each word below.

1. insignificance   **2.** figurative   **3.** originate

_____   _____   _____

C. Write a sentence to answer each question.

1. What are some of the things colors often **symbolize** in literature?

_____

2. Why might you read more than one **version** of a story?

_____

180 Essential Vocabulary Words for 6th Grade © 2009 by Linda Ward Beech, Scholastic Teaching Resources

READING/LITERATURE

Name _____ Date _____

Play the Out and Over Game.

Find a word in box 1 that does not have the same meaning as the other three words. Move that word to box 2 by writing it on the blank line. Follow the arrows and continue until you reach box 10. Complete the sentence in that box.

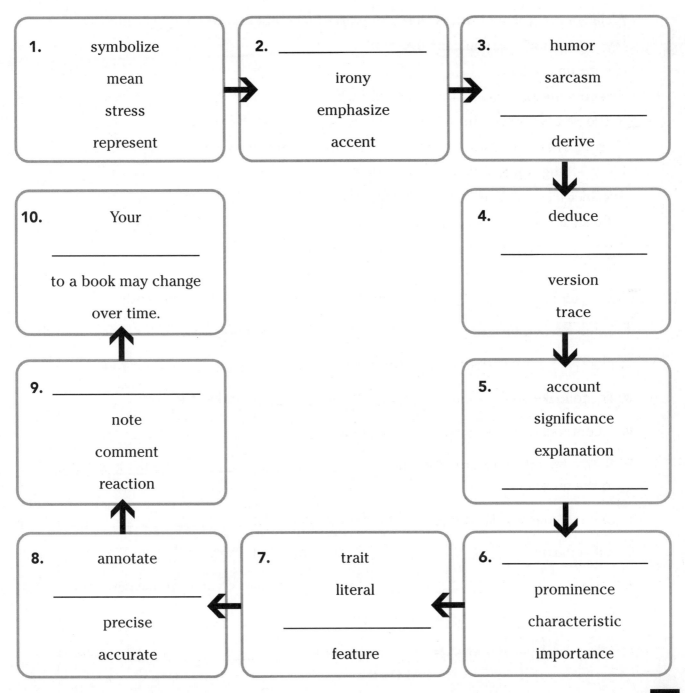

1.   symbolize

        mean

        stress

        represent

2. _____

        irony

        emphasize

        accent

3.   humor

        sarcasm

        _____

        derive

4.   deduce

        _____

        version

        trace

5.   account

        significance

        explanation

        _____

6. _____

        prominence

        characteristic

        importance

7.   trait

        literal

        _____

        feature

8.   annotate

        _____

        precise

        accurate

9. _____

        note

        comment

        reaction

10.   Your

        _____

        to a book may change

        over time.

Name _____ Date _____

clause	conceive	critique	effective	passive
plagiarize	plausible	succinct	thesis	transition

✳ SOME WORDS ARE USEFUL TO KNOW BECAUSE THEY RELATE TO WRITING.

A **clause** is a group of words that form part of a compound or complex sentence.

If you form an idea, you **conceive** of it.

A **critique** is a review.

Effective means "having the intended purpose."

In the **passive** voice, the subject receives the action of the verb.

To **plagiarize** is to use someone else's writing as your own.

If something is **plausible**, it seems likely.

Succinct means "clearly expressed in a few words."

A **thesis** is a proposition supported by an argument.

A **transition** is a change from one thing to another.

Use what you know. Write the best vocabulary word to complete each sentence.

1. Caleb needed time to _____ of a good idea for his story.

2. The teacher reminded the class not to _____ their reports.

3. Try to make your captions _____ and to the point.

4. A compound sentence has two independent _____ .

5. Notice how the author makes the _____ from one paragraph to the next.

6. Choose your words carefully so that your argument is _____ .

7. Ask a partner to _____ your first draft.

8. State your _____ at the beginning of your persuasive essay.

9. Make sure that the actions of your characters are _____ .

10. "They were given books" is an example of the _____ voice.

180 Essential Vocabulary Words for 6th Grade © 2009 by Linda Ward Beech, Scholastic Teaching Resources

WRITING

Name _____ Date _____

clause	conceive	critique	effective	passive
plagiarize	plausible	succinct	thesis	transition

A. Read the words in each row. Cross out the word that does not have a meaning that is similar to the others.

1. succinct	subtle	concise	terse
2. plausible	possible	acceptable	ridiculous
3. critique	commentary	review	crinkle
4. effective	effectual	eventual	operative
5. transition	passage	conclusion	transfer
6. conceive	conceit	originate	form
7. plagiarize	copy	recognize	steal

B. Read each question. Choose the best answer.

1. Which type of sentence has a **clause**?

❒ simple   ❒ complex   ❒ exclamatory

2. Which one has a **thesis**?

❒ essay   ❒ letter   ❒ poem

3. Which verb form is **passive**?

❒ is eating   ❒ was eaten   ❒ has eaten

Portfolio Page

Write three sentences with dependent or independent clauses in them.
Use at least three vocabulary words from this lesson.

180 Essential Vocabulary Words for 6th Grade © 2009 by Linda Ward Beech, Scholastic Teaching Resources

Name _____ Date _____

clause	conceive	critique	effective	passive
plagiarize	plausible	succinct	thesis	transition

A. Add one of these prefixes meaning "not" to each lesson word below. Then use the new word in a sentence. Check a dictionary if needed.

in-   im-

1. passive _____

_____

2. effective _____

_____

3. plausible _____

_____

B. Some words have more than one meaning. Choose the word that gives the best meaning for the underlined word in each sentence. Use a dictionary if necessary.

1. The landlord added a <u>clause</u> to the lease about pets.   ❒ provision   ❒ phrase   ❒ warning

2. She wrote a <u>thesis</u> for her college degree.   ❒ theme   ❒ thesaurus   ❒ dissertation

C. Write a sentence to answer each question.

1. How can a **critique** of written work help you?

_____

2. What advice would you give to someone about **plagiarizing**?

_____

3. What are some words that writers use to make **transitions** between paragraphs?

_____

4. When might it be useful to write in a **succinct** way?

_____

5. How does a writer **conceive** of a story?

_____

180 Essential Vocabulary Words for 6th Grade © 2009 by Linda Ward Beech, Scholastic Teaching Resources

Name _____ Date _____

Play the Word Clue Game.

Write a vocabulary word for each clue. Use each word only once.

Clues	Vocabulary Words
1. means the opposite of *verbose*	
2. can also mean "inactive"	
3. is a homophone for *claws*	
4. is a French word originally from the Greek word *kritike*	
5. the plural form is *theses*	
6. comes from the Latin word *plagiarius*, meaning "kidnapping"	
7. rhymes with *defective*	
8. can also mean "to imagine"	
9. is an antonym for *unlikely*	
10. has the words *ran* and *sit* in it	

COMMUNICATION

Name _____ Date _____

articulate	assert	assume	contradict	converse
disclose	imply	intervene	media	speculate

✱ SOME WORDS ARE USEFUL BECAUSE THEY REFER TO COMMUNICATION.

If you **articulate** something, you express it clearly.

Assert means "to state positively."

To **assume** is to take for granted.

If you **contradict** something, you say the opposite.

To **converse** is to talk informally with someone.

Disclose means "to expose."

If you **imply** something, you express it indirectly.

If you **intervene**, you come between two people or groups.

Media refers to forms of mass communication such as newspapers.

To **speculate** is to think deeply about something.

Use what you know. Write the best vocabulary word to complete each sentence.

1. Noor and Clyde like to _____ quietly at lunchtime.

2. Mr. Kelly had to _____ when the boys' voices rose.

3. Don't always _____ that you know what someone else is thinking.

4. Sometimes the _____ gives gossip as well as news.

5. Alex _____ his position in no uncertain terms.

6. Did anyone dare to _____ the speaker's point of view?

7. Laila was able to _____ clearly what the group wanted.

8. Before returning the doctor's call, Derrick _____ on what his tests results would be.

9. What did Lee mean to _____ by that remark?

10. Did this article _____ any new information on the crime?

180 Essential Vocabulary Words for 6th Grade © 2009 by Linda Ward Beech, Scholastic Teaching Resources

COMMUNICATION

Name _____ Date _____

articulate	assert	assume	contradict	converse
disclose	imply	intervene	media	speculate

A. Read the vocabulary word. Find and circle two words in that row with similar meanings.

1. assert	review	claim	question	insist
2. imply	impair	reform	suggest	hint
3. speculate	ponder	meddle	prepare	reflect
4. disclose	design	uncover	discount	divulge
5. contradict	oppose	deny	contact	implant
6. assume	mend	suppose	assure	surmise
7. articulate	whisper	arrange	verbalize	vocalize

B. Read each question. Choose the best answer.

1. Which is a reason to **intervene**? ❑ aggravate ❑ radiate ❑ mediate

2. Which one is part of the **media**? ❑ magnetism ❑ magazine ❑ magnolia

3. How might you **converse**? ❑ telephone ❑ television ❑ conversion

Portfolio Page

Write a dialogue in which you communicate with a friend. Use at least three vocabulary words from this lesson.

180 Essential Vocabulary Words for 6th Grade © 2009 by Linda Ward Beech, Scholastic Teaching Resources

Name _____ Date _____

| articulate | assert | assume | contradict | converse |
| disclose | imply | intervene | media | speculate |

A. Some words have more than one meaning. Choose the word that gives the best meaning for the vocabulary word in each sentence. Use a dictionary if needed.

1. She **assumed** a new name.   ❏ adopted   ❏ presumed   ❏ requested

2. Will they **intervene** in the
   affairs of another country?   ❏ interrupt   ❏ interfere   ❏ dabble

3. He **speculates** in the stock market.   ❏ gambles   ❏ ponders   ❏ specializes

B. Write a vocabulary word that is an antonym for each word below.

1. hide   2. agree   3. mumble

   _____   _____   _____

C. Write a sentence to answer each question.

1. When might you **assert** yourself in a group?

   _____

2. What do students your age usually **converse** about?

   _____

3. What might someone **imply** by the way he or she dresses?

   _____

4. What is an important role of the **media**?

   _____

180 Essential Vocabulary Words for 6th Grade © 2009 by Linda Ward Beech, Scholastic Teaching Resources

COMMUNICATION

Name _____ Date _____

Riddle: What can you hold without touching it?

Read each clue. Write the correct vocabulary word in each set of boxes. Then, write the letters from the shaded boxes in order on the lines below to answer the riddle.

1. express something clearly

2. reveal

3. act as a mediator

4. talk together

5. television is one example

6. state positively

7. take for granted

8. reflect upon something

9. say the opposite

10. express indirectly

Answer: __ __ __ __ __ __ __ __ __ __ __ __ *o* *n*

MATH/ECONOMICS

Name _____ Date _____

calculation	capacity	capitalism	distribution	financial
produce	proportion	revenue	splurge	statistics

✱ YOU USE CERTAIN WORDS WHEN YOU TALK ABOUT MATH OR ECONOMICS.

A **calculation** is a computation.

Capacity is how much something can hold or receive.

Capitalism is an economic system with a free market.

A **distribution** is an allotment.

A **financial** transaction has to do with money.

When a factory makes something, it **produce**s it.

Proportion is a part in relation to the whole.

Revenue is income.

If you **splurge**, you spend a lot of money.

Statistics are collected data.

Use what you know. Write the best vocabulary word to complete each sentence.

1. A _____ of each sale at the store goes to pay the rent.

2. If there is a profit, the company will make a _____ to each investor.

3. Irene spent all her savings and _____ on new shoes.

4. The company's _____ has increased in the last six months due to good sales.

5. Before she bid at the auction, Robin made a quick _____ about how much the earrings were worth.

6. Carl is paid by the number of items he _____ each day.

7. The population and income _____ indicate that this is a good place for a new mall.

8. Private ownership is one feature of _____ .

9. What is the _____ of this delivery truck?

10. The Atwells talked to a consultant about their _____ affairs.

180 Essential Vocabulary Words for 6th Grade © 2009 by Linda Ward Beech, Scholastic Teaching Resources

Name _____ Date _____

calculation	capacity	capitalism	distribution	financial
produce	proportion	revenue	splurge	statistics

A. In each sentence, circle the vocabulary word and its synonym.

1. The factory manufactured more goods last year than it **produced** this year.

2. Did this month's income exceed last month's **revenues**?

3. By Ahmet's reckoning, they could afford a new sofa, but Kamil's **calculations** didn't support the idea.

4. Elvia tried to make the **distribution** of food fair so that each family got an equal allotment.

5. The monetary crisis caused a panic in **financial** circles.

6. A **proportion** of the workers got raises, but a larger part did not.

B. Read each question. Choose the best answer.

1. Which are **statistics**? ❒ letters ❒ numbers ❒ symbols

2. Which has the most **capacity**? ❒ teacup ❒ teaspoon ❒ tablespoon

3. What's a goal of **capitalism**? ❒ losses ❒ profits ❒ savings

4. What describes a **splurge**? ❒ extravagant ❒ moderate ❒ limited

Portfolio Page

Write an entry in an expense journal explaining how you get and spend money. Use at least three vocabulary words from this lesson.

Name _____ Date _____

| calculation | capacity | capitalism | distribution | financial |
| produce | proportion | revenue | splurge | statistics |

A. Write the base word for each vocabulary word below. Then, write a sentence using the base word.

1. distribution _____

_____

2. financial _____

_____

3. capitalism _____

_____

4. calculation _____

_____

B. Write a vocabulary word that is an antonym for each word below.

1. consume   **2.** save   **3.** expenditure

_____   _____   _____

C. Underline the best ending for each sentence.

1. Statistics help census takers plan for the _____ .

     a. present   **b.** past   **c.** future

2. The largest **proportion** of most people's incomes goes for _____ .

     a. luxuries   **b.** necessities   **c.** gifts

3. They had to determine the **capacity** of the auditorium to know how many _____ .

     a. tickets to sell   **b.** lights to use   **c.** breaks to have

180 Essential Vocabulary Words for 6th Grade © 2009 by Linda Ward Beech, Scholastic Teaching Resources

MATH/ECONOMICS

Name _____ Date _____

Read the clues. Identify the correct vocabulary word and write it next to its clue. Then, find and circle each word in the puzzle.

B	D	F	K	M	P	C	J	S	W	C	H	U
C	A	L	C	U	L	A	T	I	O	N	P	Y
P	G	F	Q	I	A	P	D	K	N	R	R	K
R	D	I	S	T	R	I	B	U	T	I	O	N
O	H	N	V	G	P	T	N	Z	S	X	D	H
P	L	A	C	A	P	A	C	I	T	Y	U	O
O	T	N	E	S	P	L	U	R	G	E	C	U
R	X	C	M	Y	J	I	B	H	L	D	E	L
T	J	I	T	A	E	S	V	O	S	Q	M	I
I	C	A	C	G	K	M	P	N	V	Q	T	Z
O	I	L	S	T	A	T	I	S	T	I	C	S
N	B	F	R	E	V	E	N	U	E	W	F	J

Hint: The words can run ACROSS or DOWN.

Clues

1. an estimation _____

2. amount that an arena can hold _____

3. information collected in numerical form _____

4. related to money _____

5. an economic system with a free market _____

6. what manufacturers do _____

7. to spend exuberantly _____

8. corporate income _____

9. a fraction of the whole _____

10. allocation _____

SIZE AND AMOUNT

Name _____ Date _____

adequate	**ample**	**diminish**	**equivalent**	**extensive**
fragment	**magnitude**	**massive**	**minimal**	**quorum**

✱ YOU USE CERTAIN WORDS WHEN TALKING ABOUT SIZE AND AMOUNTS.

Adequate means "enough."

If something is **ample**, there is plenty of it.

To **diminish** is to become smaller.

If one thing is equal in value or measure to something else, it is **equivalent**.

An **extensive** area is very large.

A **fragment** is a piece of a whole.

Magnitude is the greatness of something or someone.

Something that is large and heavy is **massive**.

If you do a **minimal** amount of work, you do the smallest amount.

A **quorum** is the number of people, usually a majority, needed for a group to do business.

Use what you know. Write the best vocabulary word to complete each sentence.

1. The visitors could not get over the size of the _____ elephant.

2. You won't be hungry for long, because this restaurant serves _____ portions.

3. Jenna took a _____ of the fabric to the paint store to match the color.

4. The new park will serve many people and cover an _____ amount of land.

5. Be sure to come to the meeting so we'll have a _____ for voting.

6. When it's very hot, Mr. Rios does only a _____ amount of gardening.

7. Ms. Tucker decided not to shop; she had _____ supplies for the weekend.

8. Four cups are the _____ of a quart.

9. Kirk couldn't believe the _____ of his success.

26 **10.** The pile of sandwiches _____ as the guests ate lunch.

SIZE AND AMOUNT

Name _____ Date _____

| adequate | ample | diminish | equivalent | extensive |
| fragment | magnitude | massive | minimal | quorum |

A. Read the first word in each row. Circle a word in the row that is a synonym and underline a word that is an antonym.

1. massive	scrawny	missile	immense	tall
2. diminish	dwindle	expand	finish	dimension
3. adequate	admirable	appropriate	addition	insufficient
4. minimal	mimic	mineral	maximum	least
5. ample	amber	stingy	generous	sample
6. extensive	widespread	frequent	experience	confined

B. Write a vocabulary word that is the best synonym for each underlined word or phrase below.

1. Only a small <u>section</u> of the manuscript was found after the fire.   _____

2. A yard is <u>equal to</u> three feet.   _____

3. The <u>enormity</u> of the storm surprised people.   _____

4. The members of the council waited until a <u>majority</u> was present.   _____

Portfolio Page

Imagine you are a newspaper editor. Write five headlines for stories currently in the news. Use at least three vocabulary words from this lesson.

180 Essential Vocabulary Words for 6th Grade © 2009 by Linda Ward Beech, Scholastic Teaching Resources

SIZE AND AMOUNT

Name _____ Date _____

adequate	ample	diminish	equivalent	extensive
fragment	magnitude	massive	minimal	quorum

A. Write the correct part of speech for the vocabulary word in each sentence.

1. Although it wasn't large, the apartment was **adequate** for their needs. _____

2. As the traffic increased, Lana's chances of arriving on time **diminished**. _____

3. The store replaced the defective lamp with one of **equivalent** value. _____

4. The committee couldn't vote without a **quorum**. _____

5. It took several strong men to move the **massive** furniture. _____

B. Write a vocabulary word that is related to each word below. Then, write another word that is related to both words. Use a word you already know or find one in a resource.

Word	Related Vocabulary Word	Another Related Word
1. extend	_____	_____
2. minimum	_____	_____
3. magnify	_____	_____
4. amplify	_____	_____
5. fragmentary	_____	_____

180 Essential Vocabulary Words for 6th Grade © 2009 by Linda Ward Beech, Scholastic Teaching Resources

SIZE AND AMOUNT

Name _____ Date _____

Read each clue. Then write the answers in the spiral puzzle.

		2.								
			6.					7.	3.	
						9.				
	5.		10.							
		8.								
1.						4.				

Start

Clues

1. to lessen

2. far reaching

3. a small bit

4. opposite of insufficient

5. abundant or plentiful

6. the number of people needed for making a group decision

7. the same as

8. greatness

9. the least amount

10. large, solid, and bulky

Name _____ Date _____

convention	dispute	domestic	ethics	justify
license	panel	reside	site	welfare

✳ YOU USE CERTAIN WORDS WHEN YOU ARE STUDYING SOCIAL STUDIES.

A **convention** is a formal meeting.

When you **dispute** something, you question it.

Something **domestic** is related to a home or household.

Ethics are standards of right and wrong conduct.

If you **justify** something, you show or prove it to be right.

A **license** is a document that gives legal permission to do something.

A **panel** is a group of people who gather to discuss or decide something.

When you **reside** in a place, you live there.

A **site** is the place where something is located.

Welfare means "well-being."

Use what you know. Write the best vocabulary word to complete each sentence.

1. Joan went to see the _____ where the new school would be.

2. People expect good _____ in those elected to a government office.

3. It's illegal to drive a car without a _____ .

4. Our teacher will be attending a _____ next week.

5. In what state do you _____ ?

6. The neighbors _____ where the property line was.

7. The governor formed a _____ to study pollution from the river.

8. Jasmine was sure of her decision and didn't feel she had to _____ it.

9. Parents are responsible for the _____ of their children.

10. The twins did their _____ chores before going to the park.

180 Essential Vocabulary Words for 6th Grade © 2009 by Linda Ward Beech, Scholastic Teaching Resources

SOCIAL STUDIES

Name _____ Date _____

convention	dispute	domestic	ethics	justify
license	panel	reside	site	welfare

A. Read the words in each row. Cross out the word that does not have a meaning that is similar to the others.

1. reside	resist	dwell	live
2. convention	meeting	assembly	contention
3. dispute	argue	quarrel	discourage
4. ethics	etiquette	values	standards
5. site	location	sight	place
6. license	permit	certificate	library
7. justify	prove	jostle	validate
8. welfare	welcome	prosperity	well-being

B. Read each question. Choose the best answer.

1. Which task is **domestic**?   ❑ welding   ❑ performing   ❑ sweeping

2. Which one is a **panel**?   ❑ jury   ❑ individual   ❑ throng

Portfolio Page

Write an ad for your social studies textbook. Use at least three vocabulary words from this lesson.

Name _____ Date _____

convention	**dispute**	**domestic**	**ethics**	**justify**
license	**panel**	**reside**	**site**	**welfare**

A. Read the word meaning in each sentence. Then, write a vocabulary word that comes from the Greek or Latin word.

1. The Latin word *residere* means "to sit back." _____

2. The Latin word *convenire* means "to come together." _____

3. The Latin word *disputare* means "to reckon or discuss." _____

4. The Greek word *ethos* means "moral custom." _____

5. The Latin word *justificare* means "to do justice toward." _____

B. Some words have more than one meaning. Choose the word or phrase that gives the best meaning for the vocabulary word as it's used in each sentence.

1. A cow is not a wild animal but a **domestic** one.　❒ homelike　❒ tame　❒ shy

2. You do not have the **license** to destroy the property of others.　❒ freedom　❒ knowledge　❒ permit

3. He removed the **panel** to make repairs behind the wall.　❒ group　❒ paint　❒ board

4. The state offers **welfare** to people needing aid.　❒ public relief　❒ happiness　❒ good health

5. Go to his Web **site** to learn more.　❒ online page　❒ e-mail　❒ situation

SOCIAL STUDIES

Name _____ Date _____

Play the Hidden Word Game.

Fill out the chart with a smaller word or words that can be found in each vocabulary word. Look for words that are five letters or less. If you can find other words, add more boxes to the chart. Use a dictionary to check your answers.

Example: In **capacity**, you can find three words: *cap*, *city*, and *it*.

1. ethics				
2. reside				
3. dispute				
4. site				
5. license				
6. justify				
7. panel				
8. convention				
9. domestic				
10. welfare				

Name _____ Date _____

controversy	distort	dynasty	estate	liberate
nationalism	neutral	radical	regime	successor

✱ SOME WORDS ARE USEFUL WHEN YOU ARE TALKING ABOUT POLITICAL MATTERS.

A **controversy** is a dispute that is often lengthy and public.

If you **distort** something, you twist it out of shape.

In a **dynasty**, rulers from the same family hold power for several generations.

An **estate** is a large piece of land with a sizeable house on it.

Liberate means "to set free."

Nationalism is devotion to a country, which can sometimes be extreme.

If you are **neutral**, you don't take sides in a matter.

When something is taken to the farthest limit, it is said to be **radical**.

A **regime** is an administration.

A **successor** is someone who comes next.

Use what you know. Write the best vocabulary word to complete each sentence.

1. He is a member of the ruling _____ and the fourth family member to serve.

2. During a war, people's feelings of _____ are strong.

3. The newspapers covered the shocking _____ on a daily basis.

4. Dr. Mason is the _____ to our principal, who is retiring.

5. Vince is an original thinker and sometimes has _____ ideas.

6. Does this ad _____ the facts?

7. Although many people expressed strong points of view, Dean remained

_____ .

8. Their _____ includes a mansion and 100 acres.

9. When the dictator was toppled, a new _____ took over.

10. They hoped to _____ those who were captured.

180 Essential Vocabulary Words for 6th Grade, Scholastic Teaching Resources

SOCIAL STUDIES/POLITICAL

Name _____ Date _____

controversy	distort	dynasty	estate	liberate
nationalism	neutral	radical	regime	successor

A. Circle the two synonyms in each sentence.

1. The radical group had several rather extreme ideas.

2. The wrangling continued for weeks until the controversy was finally settled.

3. Amina felt that the politician misrepresented and distorted the issue.

4. It is important that a judge remain impartial and neutral.

5. Rescue workers tried to liberate the man from the wreckage, but it was hours before they could release him.

6. Under Patrick's regime, the management of the company improved.

7. Viewers applauded exhibits of nationalism and patriotism at the parade.

B. Read each question. Choose the best answer.

1. Which one is a **successor**? ❏ first ❏ last ❏ next

2. Who is in a **dynasty**? ❏ family ❏ friends ❏ neighbors

3. What describes an **estate**? ❏ grant ❏ gray ❏ grand

Portfolio Page

Write a page of dialogue for a TV talk show about a political situation. Use at least three vocabulary words from this lesson.

SOCIAL STUDIES/POLITICAL

Name _____ Date _____

| controversy | distort | dynasty | estate | liberate |
| nationalism | neutral | radical | regime | successor |

A. Underline the best ending for each sentence.

1. A **controversy** usually arises because people _____.

        a. tend to agree   **b.** don't care   **c.** strongly disagree

2. People who own **estates** are usually _____.

        a. unemployed   **b.** wealthy   **c.** destitute

3. People exhibit **nationalism** when they _____.

        a. cheer at ballgames   **b.** salute the flag   **c.** watch television

B. Write a vocabulary word that is an antonym for each word below.

1. opinionated   **2.** imprison   **3.** moderate

_____   _____   _____

C. Write a sentence to answer each question.

1. Why does information on the Internet sometimes get **distorted**?

_____

2. What ancient civilizations were ruled by **dynasties**?

_____

3. How are **successors** to government offices chosen in the United States?

_____

4. Why might people want a change in a **regime**?

_____

Name _____ Date _____

Play the Word Clue Game.

Write a vocabulary word for each clue.

Clues	Vocabulary Words
1. can describe a color such as beige	
2. is an antonym for *confine*	
3. is a synonym for *drastic*	
4. is a form of the word *regimen*	
5. comes from the Greek word *dunastes,* meaning "ruler"	
6. can also refer to all of the possessions of someone who is diseased	
7. is related to the words *succession* and *succeed*	
8. has the words *on* and *rove* in it	
9. can also mean "warp" or "deform"	
10. is related to the words *nation, national, nationality,* and *nationalize*	

180 Essential Vocabulary Words for 6th Grade © 2009 by Linda Ward Beech, Scholastic Teaching Resources

Name _____ Date _____

displace	formulate	hereditary	hypothesize	inquiry
nuclear	specify	theory	trajectory	verify

✱ YOU USE CERTAIN WORDS WHEN YOU TALK ABOUT SCIENCE.

To **displace** is to take the place of something.

If you **formulate** something, you plan it.

Something that is **hereditary** is passed along biologically.

When you **hypothesize**, you put forth an explanation
for further investigation.

An **inquiry** is a request for information.

Something that is **nuclear** has energy from atoms.

Specify means "to state clearly."

A **theory** is an assumption or idea based on knowledge.

A **trajectory** is the path of a moving body.

If you **verify** something, you prove that it is true.

Use what you know. Write the best vocabulary word to complete each sentence.

1. Their eyes followed the _____ of the rocket.

2. Some of the country's electricity comes from _____ power plants.

3. A boat _____ water when it is launched into a harbor.

4. Blue eyes are a _____ trait.

5. Before conducting his experiment, Leo _____ what the outcome
might be.

6. Please _____ the equipment you will need for the field trip.

7. Alice _____ a plan for her science presentation.

8. You can _____ when it will be high tide by checking in the newspaper.

9. Kitty had a _____ about why the fish weren't eating.

10. The botanist answered our _____ about why leaves turn colors
in the fall.

180 Essential Vocabulary Words for 6th Grade © 2009 by Linda Ward Beech, Scholastic Teaching Resources

Name _____ Date _____

displace	formulate	hereditary	hypothesize	inquiry
nuclear	specify	theory	trajectory	verify

A. Write a vocabulary word that is a synonym for each underlined word or words in the sentences.

1. Their <u>investigation</u> will take several weeks. _____

2. Is the color of your hair <u>inherited</u>? _____

3. The new computer will <u>replace</u> the one we have now. _____

4. Jamie will <u>devise</u> a schedule for feeding the animals. _____

5. The report should <u>state exactly</u> the steps needed for the procedure. _____

6. Astronomers monitored the <u>path</u> of the shooting star. _____

7. Vic <u>conjectured</u> about how the mouse got out of its cage. _____

8. Can you <u>confirm</u> the results of the experiment? _____

B. Read each question. Choose the best answer.

1. Which one is a **theory**? ❑ hypocrite ❑ hippopotamus ❑ hypothesis

2. Which one could be **nuclear**? ❑ submarine ❑ substitute ❑ subcontinent

Portfolio Page

Write a report about a science experiment you have done. Use at least three vocabulary words from this lesson.

SCIENCE

Name _____ Date _____

displace	**formulate**	**hereditary**	**hypothesize**	**inquiry**
nuclear	**specify**	**theory**	**trajectory**	**verify**

A. **Write the correct part of speech for the vocabulary word in each sentence.**

1. She had to **formulate** a strategy for playing
on the team and finishing her daily homework. _____

2. Certain diseases are **hereditary**. _____

3. The professor responded to their **inquiry** in her letter. _____

4. Do the instructions **specify** how much water we should add? _____

5. Beezy brought her ID card to **verify** that she worked in the lab. _____

6. Many submarines run on **nuclear** power. _____

B. **Read the word meaning in each sentence. Then, write a vocabulary word that comes from each Greek or Latin word.**

1. The Latin word *trajectus* means "throw across." _____

2. The Greek word *hupothesis* means "proposal." _____

3. The Greek word *theoros* means "contemplation." _____

C. **Substitute these prefixes for the prefix *dis-* in *displace*. Then, write a sentence using each new word.**

mis- 1. _____place

_____

re- 2. _____place

_____

180 Essential Vocabulary Words for 6th Grade © 2009 by Linda Ward Beech, Scholastic Teaching Resources

Name _____ Date _____

Analogy

An analogy is a comparison based on how things are related to one another. Decide how the first set of words is related. Then, use the best vocabulary word from this lesson to complete each of these analogies.

1. Distort is to warp as

supplant is to ___ ___ ___ ___ ___ ___ ___ ___ .

2. Succeed is to successor as

inquire is to ___ ___ ___ ___ ___ ___ ___ .

3. Justify is to justification as

___ ___ ___ ___ ___ ___ ___ is to specification.

4. Disprove is to prove as

refute is to ___ ___ ___ ___ ___ ___ .

5. Symbol is to symbolize as

formula is to ___ ___ ___ ___ ___ ___ ___ ___ ___ .

6. Adequate is to enough as

inherited is to ___ ___ ___ ___ ___ ___ ___ ___ ___ ___ .

7. Dwindle is to diminish as

guess is to ___ ___ ___ ___ ___ ___ ___ ___ ___ ___ .

8. Oil is to furnace as

___ ___ ___ ___ ___ ___ ___ is to reactor.

9. A fragment is to a piece as

an idea is to a ___ ___ ___ ___ ___ ___ .

10. A calculation is to an estimation as

a route is to a ___ ___ ___ ___ ___ ___ ___ ___ .

STUDY SKILLS

Name _____ Date _____

approach	attain	consequence	differentiate	logical
reinforce	relevant	routine	supplement	synthesize

✳ YOU USE CERTAIN WORDS WHEN TALKING ABOUT STUDY SKILLS.

When you **approach** a subject, you start to work on it.

If you **attain** good skills, you gain them.

A **consequence** is a result.

Differentiate means "to find differences."

If something is **logical**, it's reasonable.

Reinforce means "to strengthen."

When something is **relevant**, it is connected to the subject.

Something that is **routine** is regular.

A **supplement** is something that is added to make a work larger or more complete.

When you **synthesize**, you put parts or elements together.

Use what you know. Write the best vocabulary word to complete each sentence.

1. It's a good idea to make studying a _____ activity.

2. Rereading certain passages in a text can _____ your understanding of a subject.

3. Good readers try to focus on _____ facts in a text.

4. If you _____ studying in a positive way, it can make a difference.

5. Students need to _____ a level of proficiency in a subject.

6. The _____ of not completing assignments is often reflected in low grades.

7. After learning facts, students need to _____ information in a meaningful way.

8. There are various purposes for writing, and students must learn to _____ among them.

9. A _____ offers more information about a subject.

42 **10.** Students often ask themselves: Does this make sense? Is it _____?

Name _____ Date _____

| approach | attain | consequence | differentiate | logical |
| reinforce | relevant | routine | supplement | synthesize |

A. Read the words in each group. Write a vocabulary word that means the same or almost the same thing.

1. acquire, reach _____

2. pertinent, associated _____

3. sensible, reasonable _____

4. result, outcome _____

5. usual, customary _____

6. distinguish, discriminate _____

B. Read each question. Choose the best answer.

1. What might you **approach**? ❐ homework ❐ homesick ❐ homemade

2. What might you **reinforce**? ❐ frills ❐ drills ❐ skills

3. What might you **synthesize**? ❐ chaplains ❐ chaperones ❐ chapters

4. Which one is a **supplement**? ❐ appendix ❐ caption ❐ apprentice

Portfolio Page

Write a set of guidelines for good study habits. Use at least three vocabulary words from this lesson.

STUDY SKILLS

Name _____ Date _____

approach	attain	consequence	differentiate	logical
reinforce	relevant	routine	supplement	synthesize

A. A suffix has been added to each lesson word below. Underline the suffix in each word. Then, write what part of speech the word is. Use a dictionary if needed.

1. routinely _____

2. reinforcement _____

3. supplemental _____

4. approachable _____

5. attainment _____

B. A prefix has been added to each lesson word below. Underline the prefix in each word. Then, write a sentence using the word. Use a dictionary if needed.

1. illogical _____

_____

2. irrelevant _____

_____

C. Write a sentence to answer each question.

1. Why is it important to **synthesize** information?

_____

2. What is a **consequence** of poor study skills?

_____

3. How do you **differentiate** facts from opinions?

_____

180 Essential Vocabulary Words for 6th Grade © 2009 by Linda Ward Beech, Scholastic Teaching Resources

Name _____ Date _____

Play the Out and Over Game.

Find a word in box 1 that does not have the same meaning as the other three words. Move that word to box 2 by writing it on the blank line. Follow the arrows and continue until you reach box 10. Complete the sentence in that box with the last word you moved.

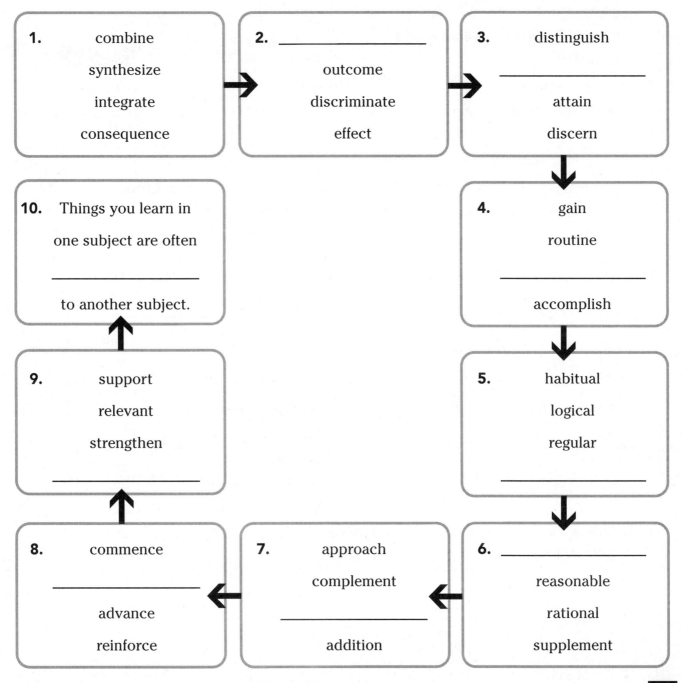

1. combine
   synthesize
   integrate
   consequence

2. _____
   outcome
   discriminate
   effect

3. distinguish
   _____
   attain
   discern

4. gain
   routine
   _____
   accomplish

5. habitual
   logical
   regular
   _____

6. _____
   reasonable
   rational
   supplement

7. approach
   complement
   _____
   addition

8. commence
   _____
   advance
   reinforce

9. support
   relevant
   strengthen
   _____

10. Things you learn in one subject are often _____ to another subject.

Name _____ Date _____

anticipate	credible	crucial	distinguish	ensure
interpretation	optional	potential	relate	relax

✱ SOME WORDS ARE USEFUL TO KNOW FOR TEST-TAKING.

If you **anticipate** something, you think it will happen.

A **credible** statement is believable.

Crucial means "very important."

When you **distinguish** things, you tell them apart.

When you **ensure** something, you guarantee or make certain of it.

An **interpretation** is an explanation.

Something **optional** is not required.

Potential means "might actually happen."

If you **relate** things, you connect them in thought or meaning.

To **relax** is to lessen in intensity.

Use what you know. Write the best vocabulary word to complete each sentence.

1. A good tip to follow when beginning a test is to _____ .

2. It's a good idea to _____ the kind of questions that will be asked.

3. Being prepared is _____ for taking a test.

4. Studying helps _____ students will do well.

5. Some questions ask for an _____ of a statement.

6. Other questions call for students to _____ between two points of view.

7. For an essay question, try to show how events _____ to one another.

8. Tests are just one tool used to assess a student's _____ success.

9. Be sure your responses are _____ by including evidence or examples.

10. If you have time, try to answer any _____ questions.

180 Essential Vocabulary Words for 6th Grade © 2009 by Linda Ward Beech, Scholastic Teaching Resources

Name _____ Date _____

anticipate	credible	crucial	distinguish	ensure
interpretation	optional	potential	relate	relax

A. Write a vocabulary word that is a synonym for the underlined word in each sentence.

1. Many students don't realize their <u>possible</u> skills.   _____

2. The question asked for an <u>explication</u> of the king's actions.   _____

3. Poppy checked to make sure her answers were <u>plausible</u>.   _____

4. In Martha's essay, she <u>associated</u> the furniture people used to the clothing they wore in that period.   _____

5. Abbie thought carefully as she tried to <u>detect</u> the differences in the excerpts.   _____

6. Noel felt it was <u>critical</u> to get enough sleep before a test.   _____

7. Nina's hand was tired from writing so she <u>loosened</u> her grip on the pencil.   _____

8. Miles arrived early to <u>guarantee</u> that he would not miss any instructions before the test.   _____

B. Read each question. Choose the best answer.

1. What might you **anticipate**?   ❐ the present   ❐ the past   ❐ the future

2. Which one is **optional**?   ❐ elective   ❐ mandatory   ❐ obligatory

Portfolio Page

Imagine that you write fortunes for a fortune cookie factory. Write three to five fortunes about test-taking. Use at least three vocabulary words from this lesson.

Name _____ Date _____

anticipate	credible	crucial	distinguish	ensure
interpretation	optional	potential	relate	relax

A. Write an antonym for each of the vocabulary words below. Use a dictionary if needed.

1. credible _____

2. optional _____

3. crucial _____

4. relax _____

5. distinguish _____

B. Write a vocabulary word that is related to each word below. Then, write another word that is related to both words. Use a word you already know or find one in a resource.

Word	Related Vocabulary Word	Another Related Word
1. interpret	_____	_____
2. anticipatory	_____	_____
3. relationship	_____	_____

C. Write a sentence to answer each question.

1. What **potential** strengths do you have?

_____

2. What do you think is the best way to **ensure** good test results?

_____

180 Essential Vocabulary Words for 6th Grade © 2009 by Linda Ward Beech, Scholastic Teaching Resources

Name _____ Date _____

Riddle: What kind of cup won't hold water?

To answer the riddle, find and shade the spaces with word pairs that are synonyms.

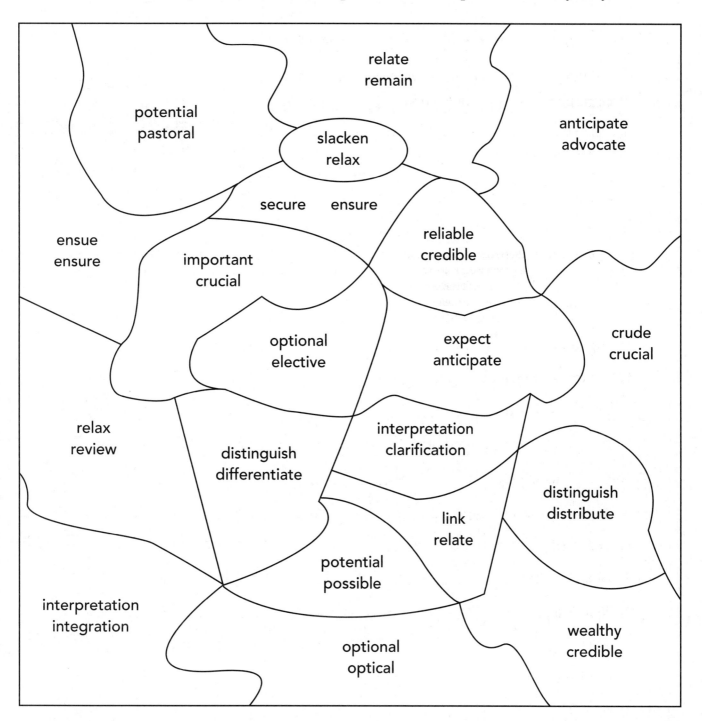

Answer: _____

Name _____ Date _____

complex	**component**	**concept**	**criteria**	**enhance**
generate	**impact**	**innovation**	**perceive**	**scheme**

✱ YOU USE CERTAIN WORDS WHEN TALKING ABOUT ART.

A painting that is **complex** has interwoven parts.

A **component** is a part of a whole.

A **concept** is an idea.

Criteria are standards.

If you **enhance** something, you make it better.

When you **generate** something, you bring it into existence.

Impact is the effect one thing has on another.

An **innovation** is something new.

When you **perceive** something, you see or become aware of it.

A **scheme** is a system.

Use what you know. Write the best vocabulary word to complete each sentence.

1. The class brainstormed to _____ ideas for the poster.

2. Allie's design was _____ and had many interconnected parts.

3. The stark lines of the sculpture had a big _____ on viewers.

4. Paul added shadows to _____ the figure in his painting.

5. Maya worked in a color _____ of yellows and orange.

6. Each group came up with a _____ for a hall mural.

7. An artist often _____ things differently than others do.

8. This designer is known for her creativity and _____ .

9. What _____ will the judges use in the art show?

10. The trees in the foreground are an important _____ in this work.

Name _____ Date _____

complex	component	concept	criteria	enhance
generate	impact	innovation	perceive	scheme

A. Read the words in each row. Write a vocabulary word that means the same or almost the same thing.

1. behold, view _____

2. composite, compound _____

3. improve, augment _____

4. thought, notion _____

5. element, part _____

6. produce, beget _____

7. change, novelty _____

8. impression, effect _____

B. Read each question. Choose the best answer.

1. Which one is a **scheme**? ❏ scene ❏ plot ❏ scream

2. Which are **criteria**? ❏ ruins ❏ rulers ❏ rules

Portfolio Page

Choose an artwork that you have created or that you admire. Write a review of it explaining your reaction. Use at least three vocabulary words from this lesson.

Name _____ Date _____

| complex | component | concept | criteria | enhance |
| generate | impact | innovation | perceive | scheme |

A. **Underline the best ending for each sentence.**

1. People use **criteria** as a way to _____ .

a. store art   **b.** judge art   **c.** ignore art

2. Before an art auction, the goal is to **generate** _____ .

a. materials   **b.** interest   **c.** mistakes

3. To **enhance** an artwork, museums often use special _____ .

a. lighting   **b.** doors   **c.** floors

B. **Some words have more than one meaning. Choose the word that gives the best meaning for the vocabulary word as it's used in each sentence.**

1. Lorenzo had a **complex** about
showing his artwork.   ❏ wish   ❏ thrill   ❏ fear

2. The **impact** of the crash
was severe.   ❏ blow   ❏ import   ❏ instinct

3. Bailey did not **perceive** the
problem in time to prevent it.   ❏ solve   ❏ understand   ❏ cause

C. **Write the number of syllables in each vocabulary word. Then, write the syllables that make up the word.**

Vocabulary Word	Number of Syllables	Syllables
1. component	_____	_____
2. scheme	_____	_____
3. concept	_____	_____
4. innovation	_____	_____

Name _____ Date _____

Read the clues. Complete the puzzle using vocabulary words.

1. increase or add to something

2. standards for making a judgment

3. an idea or notion

4. something newly introduced

5. a plan

6. cause or create

7. detect or see

8. intricately formed

9. an effect on someone

10. a portion or part of something

1. __ __ __ **A** __ __ __

2. __ **R** __ __ __ __ __ __

3. __ __ __ __ __ __ **T**

4. __ __ __ __ __ __ __ **I** __ __

5. **S** __ __ __ __ __

6. **G** __ __ __ __ __ __ __

7. __ __ **R** __ __ __ __ __

8. __ __ __ __ __ **E** __

9. __ __ __ **A** __ __

10. __ __ __ __ __ __ __ __ **T**

Name _____ Date _____

chronology	former	frequent	initial	instantaneous
ongoing	priority	prompt	simultaneous	subsequent

✱ YOU USE CERTAIN WORDS WHEN REFERRING TO TIME.

Chronology is the arrangement of events in time.

If something happened earlier, it happened at a **former** time.

Frequent means "often."

An **initial** step is the first one.

Instantaneous means "right away."

Something that is **ongoing** is continuing.

A **priority** is something that is urgent.

When you are on time, you are **prompt**.

Simultaneous means "at the same time."

Subsequent means "coming after."

Use what you know. Write the vocabulary word that best completes each sentence.

1. Dana always tried to be _____ for math class.

2. The class studied a lot because there were _____ tests in science.

3. The chart showed the _____ of events for that period in history.

4. Ziggy's _____ attempt at drawing his dog didn't succeed, so he tried again.

5. Although Molly was sorry to leave her _____ school, she made new friends quickly.

6. When he saw his grade, Biff's joy was _____ .

7. Completing her homework was a _____ for Carla before going to soccer practice.

8. Joel didn't get the information he wanted on his first try, but he found it on a _____ attempt.

9. The _____ ringing of the phone and the doorbell threatened to send Chandra in two different directions.

10. The students conducted an _____ experiment for the whole semester.

Name _____ Date _____

| chronology | former | frequent | initial | instantaneous |
| ongoing | priority | prompt | simultaneous | subsequent |

A. Read the first word in each row. Circle a word in the row that is a synonym and underline a word that is an antonym.

1. prompt	perfect	punctual	prom	late
2. initial	final	beginning	identical	initiation
3. subsequent	subtle	subjective	earlier	succeeding
4. frequent	always	repeatedly	seldom	never
5. instantaneous	eventual	intensive	immediate	impressive
6. ongoing	overdrive	perpetual	oncoming	limited
7. simultaneous	alternate	similar	concurrent	singular

B. Read each question. Choose the best answer.

1. Which one is a **chronology**?   ❏ timecard   ❏ time zone   ❏ timeline

2. Which one is **former**?   ❏ last year   ❏ this year   ❏ next year

3. Which one is a **priority**?   ❏ schoolyard   ❏ schoolwork   ❏ school bell

Portfolio Page

Write a diary entry that gives a chronology of your activities for a day. Use at least three vocabulary words from this lesson.

Name _____ Date _____

chronology	**former**	**frequent**	**initial**	**instantaneous**
ongoing	**priority**	**prompt**	**simultaneous**	**subsequent**

A. **Write the correct part of speech for the vocabulary word in each sentence.**

  1. The students waved at their **former** teacher. _____

  2. Carmen's **priority** was to make the basketball team. _____

  3. The boys had an **ongoing** joke about food. _____

  4. Although the team lost, the players vowed
  to win **subsequent** games. _____

B. **Read the word meaning in each sentence. Then write the vocabulary word that comes from each Latin or Greek word.**

  1. The Latin word *initialis* means "beginning." _____

  2. The Greek word *chrono* indicates time. _____

  3. The Latin word *frequens* means "full or crowded." _____

  4. The Latin word *instans* means "instant." _____

C. **Write a sentence to answer each question.**

  1. What are two **simultaneous** actions that you can perform?

  _____

  2. Why is it important to be **prompt**?

  _____

Name _____ Date _____

An analogy is a comparison based on how things are related to one another. Decide how the first set of words is related. Then, use the best vocabulary word from this lesson to complete each of these analogies.

1. Potential is to possible as

   previous is to ___ ___ ___ ___ ___ ___ .

2. Optional is to required as

   tardy is to ___ ___ ___ ___ ___ ___ .

3. License is to permit as

   order is to ___ ___ ___ ___ ___ ___ ___ ___ ___ ___ .

4. Logical is to reasonable as

   continuing is to ___ ___ ___ ___ ___ ___ ___ .

5. Effectively is to effective as

   initially is to ___ ___ ___ ___ ___ ___ ___ .

6. Literal is to figurative as

   occasional is to ___ ___ ___ ___ ___ ___ ___ ___ .

7. Passive is to active as

   delayed is to ___ ___ ___ ___ ___ ___ ___ ___ ___ ___ ___ ___ ___ .

8. Theorize is to theory as

   prioritize is to ___ ___ ___ ___ ___ ___ ___ ___ .

9. Widespread is to extensive as

   following is to ___ ___ ___ ___ ___ ___ ___ ___ ___ .

10. Credible is to believable as

    concurrent is to ___ ___ ___ ___ ___ ___ ___ ___ ___ ___ ___ .

CITIZENSHIP

Name _____ Date _____

benefit	commit	considerate	contribution	cooperation
discriminate	informed	mediate	privilege	stance

✱ SOME WORDS ARE OFTEN USED WHEN TALKING ABOUT CITIZENSHIP.

A **benefit** is something that is helpful.

When you **commit** to something, you pledge to do it.

If you are **considerate**, you think about the feelings of others.

A **contribution** is something that you give.

Cooperation is working together with others.

When you **discriminate**, you make a distinction.

If you are **informed**, you have knowledge of something.

When you **mediate**, you help opposing sides in a dispute.

A **privilege** is a special right or advantage.

A **stance** is a position that you take on an issue.

Use what you know. Write the best vocabulary word to complete each sentence.

1. A good citizen stays _____ about issues in the community.

2. Mr. Cole voted against the proposed law because he saw no _____ to it.

3. It's important to hear all sides before taking a _____ .

4. Americans enjoy the _____ of voting in free elections.

5. Morgan helped to _____ the argument so the meeting could proceed.

6. Ella has made many _____ to this committee.

7. The mayor was greatly liked by people because of his _____ manner.

8. Brewster pointed out that everyone's _____ was needed to get the project going.

9. The students thought carefully so they would not _____ against any group when they chose their mascot.

58 **10.** Ruth was _____ to turning the empty lot into a small park.

Name _____ Date _____

benefit	commit	considerate	contribution	cooperation
discriminate	informed	mediate	privilege	stance

A. In each sentence, circle the vocabulary word and its synonym.

1. Ingrid read a lot to stay informed and was very knowledgeable about the issue.

2. The captain wanted to settle the dispute, so she began to mediate between the groups.

3. Olivia was thoughtful and considerate to give up her seat on the bus.

4. His donation of time was an important contribution to the project.

5. Roland committed to working on weekends and promised to help out some evenings, too.

6. Although at first Zeke took a firm stance, Josh convinced him to change his position.

B. Read each question. Choose the best answer.

1. What happens if you **discriminate**? ❑ unfairness ❑ fairness ❑ fair-minded

2. Which one is a **benefit**? ❑ assistance ❑ limitation ❑ barrier

3. Which one is a **privilege**? ❑ advantage ❑ pledge ❑ adversity

4. Which one does not need **cooperation**? ❑ group ❑ team ❑ individual

Portfolio Page

Exercise your citizenship rights. Write a letter to the editor of a local newspaper commenting on a recent issue in the news. Explain your point of view.

180 Essential Vocabulary Words for 6th Grade © 2009 by Linda Ward Beech

CITIZENSHIP

Name _____ Date _____

| benefit | commit | considerate | contribution | cooperation |
| discriminate | informed | mediate | privilege | stance |

A. Write a vocabulary word that is related to each word below. Then, write another word that is related to both words. Use related words you already know or find words in a resource.

Word **Related Vocabulary Word** **Another Related Word**

1. beneficial _____ _____

2. contribute _____ _____

3. discriminatory _____ _____

4. mediation _____ _____

5. cooperative _____ _____

B. Write a sentence to answer each question.

1. What is a cause to which you might **commit** your time?

_____

2. What is your **stance** on school uniforms?

_____

3. Why does the **privilege** of free speech come with responsibilities?

_____

C. Write an antonym for each vocabulary word below.

1. considerate _____

2. informed _____

180 Essential Vocabulary Words for 6th Grade © 2009 by Linda Ward Beech, Scholastic Teaching Resources

CITIZENSHIP

Name _____ Date _____

Play the Hidden Word Game.

Fill out the chart with a smaller word or words that can be found in each word. Look for words that are five letters or less. If you can find other words, add more boxes to the chart. Use a dictionary to check your answers.

Example: In **priority**, you can find three words: *prior*, *or*, and *it*.

1. commit

2. privilege

3. benefit

4. stance

5. mediate

6. contribution

7. discriminate

8. cooperation

9. informed

10. considerate

180 Essential Vocabulary Words for 6th Grade © 2009 by Linda Ward Beech, Scholastic Teaching Resources

COMPETITION

Name _____ Date _____

aggressive	competitive	confront	contend	dominate
eliminate	exaggerate	exceed	oppose	pursue

✱ YOU USE CERTAIN WORDS WHEN YOU TALK ABOUT COMPETITION.

Someone who is **aggressive** is eager and bold.

If you are **competitive**, you enjoy rivalry.

When you **confront** someone, you stand face to face with that person.

Contend means "to compete."

When you **dominate**, you are in a position of power.

Eliminate means "get rid of."

If you **exaggerate**, you overstate something.

To **exceed** is to be greater than.

When you **oppose** something, you are against it.

If you **pursue** something, you go after it.

Use what you know. Write the best vocabulary word to complete each sentence.

1. Cameron was proud because he _____ his own goals in math.

2. After the tryouts, the coach will _____ several players.

3. Ariel is very _____ and loves to win.

4. The students _____ the suggestion to shorten their lunch period.

5. People who brag often _____ their claims.

6. Felix is so tall, he _____ the basketball court.

7. The shortstop _____ the runner and tagged him.

8. The goalie _____ the players who tried to score.

9. The classes will _____ with each other to see which one will raise the most money for the trip.

10. Suli was enterprising and _____ about getting permission for the club to meet before school.

Name _____ Date _____

| aggressive | competitive | confront | contend | dominate |
| eliminate | exaggerate | exceed | oppose | pursue |

A. Read the first word in each row. Circle the other words in that row with similar meanings.

1. **exceed** — surpass — excuse — proceed — outdo

2. **dominate** — domino — domestic — control — govern

3. **aggressive** — aghast — ardent — zealous — meek

4. **exaggerate** — exasperate — boast — examine — magnify

5. **eliminate** — remove — discard — elevate — embroider

6. **pursue** — punch — follow — chase — purge

7. **confront** — face — comfort — hide — encounter

B. Read each question. Choose the best answer.

1. Which means you **oppose**? ❐ neutral ❐ against ❐ for

2. Which one is **competitive**? ❐ eraser ❐ tracer ❐ racer

3. Who might **contend**? ❐ spectator ❐ contestant ❐ judge

Portfolio Page

Imagine you write an advice column for a magazine. Write a letter of advice to a reader who has trouble dealing with competition.

COMPETITION

Name _____ Date _____

aggressive	competitive	confront	contend	dominate
eliminate	exaggerate	exceed	oppose	pursue

A. Suffixes have been added to each lesson word below. Underline the suffix in each word. Then write the part of speech the word is. Use a dictionary if needed.

1. contender _____

2. domination _____

3. aggressively _____

4. competitively _____

B. Write an antonym for each vocabulary word below. Use a dictionary if needed.

1. oppose   **2. eliminate**   **3. exceed**

_____   _____   _____

C. Underline the best ending for each sentence.

1. The tennis player **pursued** the ball in order to _____ .

   a. drop it   **b.** return it   **c.** lose it

2. Ads sometimes **exaggerate** in order to _____ .

   a. try out products   **b.** win products   **c.** sell products

3. Mrs. Lowe needed to **confront** her son because he was always _____ .

   a. eating his vegetables   **b.** late for school   **c.** getting good grades

180 Essential Vocabulary Words for 6th Grade © 2009 by Linda Ward Beech, Scholastic Teaching Resources

COMPETITION

Name _____ Date _____

Read each clue. Then, write the answers in the spiral puzzle.

					3.				
								7.	
2.	6.			9.					
			10.				4.		
		8.							
1.	5.								

Start

Clues

1. going beyond your goals

2. combat or resist

3. being assertive

4. delete

5. run after

6. compete

7. stretch the truth

8. be in the most prominent position

9. come face to face with

10. enjoy rivalry

180 Essential Vocabulary Words for 6th Grade © 2009 by Linda Ward Beech, Scholastic Teaching Resources

VERBS

Name _____ Date _____

attribute	confine	construct	convey	coordinate
deny	devise	emancipate	isolate	obtain

✱ A VERB IS A WORD THAT SHOWS ACTION IN A SENTENCE. THESE VERBS ARE USEFUL TO KNOW IN SCHOOL.

If you **attribute** something, you credit it as belonging to someone.

Confine means "to limit."

When you **construct** something, you build it.

To **convey** is to take something from one place to another.

If you **coordinate** things, you organize them.

When you **deny** something, you say it isn't true.

To **devise** is to arrange in your mind.

Emancipate means "free from oppression."

If you **isolate** something, you separate it from other things.

Obtain means "get."

Use what you know. Write the best vocabulary word to complete each sentence.

1. The bus will _____ the passengers to the gate.

2. Erin will _____ the tickets for the performance.

3. The farmer had to _____ this cow from the herd because it was sick.

4. Who will _____ the arrangements for the event?

5. Mr. Hopkins _____ the party to the yard so the house wouldn't get dirty.

6. Although the box is empty, Beryl will _____ that she ate all the crackers.

7. Have you ever wondered how beavers _____ a dam?

8. A law was passed to _____ enslaved people.

9. The players _____ their successful season to the coach.

10. Chantal tried to _____ a way to leave without being noticed.

180 Essential Vocabulary Words for 6th Grade © 2009 by Linda Ward Beech, Scholastic Teaching Resources

VERBS

Name _____ Date _____

attribute	**confine**	**construct**	**convey**	**coordinate**
deny	**devise**	**emancipate**	**isolate**	**obtain**

A. Read the words in each group. Write a vocabulary word that means the same or almost the same thing.

1. restrict, limit _____

2. erect, compose _____

3. credit, ascribe _____

4. contradict, disavow _____

5. invent, contrive _____

6. free, liberate _____

7. transport, carry _____

8. acquire, gain _____

B. Read each question. Choose the best answer.

1. What might you **coordinate**? ☐ fare ☐ fair ☐ fear

2. Which one is usually **isolated**? ☐ lighthouse ☐ schoolhouse ☐ firehouse

Portfolio Page

Send a text message to a friend about a plan you have devised for a school parade. Use at least three vocabulary words from this lesson.

Name _____ Date _____

attribute	confine	construct	convey	coordinate
deny	devise	emancipate	isolate	obtain

A. Some words have more than one meaning. Choose the word that gives the best meaning for the vocabulary word as it's used in each sentence.

1. Luna's main **attribute** is loyalty.   ❑ quality   ❑ goal   ❑ assignment

2. Mr. Windsor didn't want to **deny** his dog anything.   ❑ present   ❑ refuse   ❑ feed

3. She **conveyed** her message.   ❑ convicted   ❑ opened   ❑ communicated

4. What are the **coordinates** for that location?   ❑ plans   ❑ numbers   ❑ agreements

B. Write a vocabulary word that is related to each word below. Then write another word that is related to both words. Use a word you already know or find one in a resource.

Word	Related Vocabulary Word	Another Related Word
1. constructive	_____	_____
2. emancipator	_____	_____
3. isolationism	_____	_____
4. obtainer	_____	_____

C. Write a sentence to answer each question.

1. What are two reasons you might **confine** a pet?

_____

2. Why might you **devise** an excuse for getting out of something?

_____

180 Essential Vocabulary Words for 6th Grade © 2009 by Linda Ward Beech, Scholastic Teaching Resources

Name _____ Date _____

Riddle: Where can you always find sympathy?

Read each clue. Write the correct vocabulary word in each set of boxes. Then, write the letters from the shaded boxes in order on the lines below to answer the riddle.

1. say you didn't do something

2. restrict

3. set free from bondage

4. set apart

5. invent

6. make or build

7. get possession of

8. give credit for

9. organize something

10. transport something

Answer: __ __ __ __ __ __ __ __ __ __

ADJECTIVES

Name _____ Date _____

appropriate	consistent	cumulative	dutiful	probable
sparse	subjective	trivial	universal	vital

✱ AN ADJECTIVE IS A WORD THAT MODIFIES A NOUN OR PRONOUN. THESE ADJECTIVES ARE USEFUL TO KNOW IN SCHOOL.

Appropriate means "suitable."

If you are **consistent**, you always follow the same course or pattern.

Something that increases in stages is **cumulative**.

Dutiful means being careful to perform your duty.

If something is likely to happen, it is **probable**.

Sparse means "not crowded."

Something within your mind but not observable to others is **subjective**.

Something **trivial** is of little importance.

When something is **universal**, it affects the whole world.

Vital means of "great importance."

Use what you know. Write the best vocabulary word to complete each sentence.

1. The grades given each spring were _____ over the year.

2. Attendance at the meeting was _____ ; few people came.

3. When she went hiking, Kia wanted to wear the _____ boots.

4. Uli ignored Hugo's remark because he thought it was so _____ .

5. Gert was erratic and not always _____ in her actions.

6. It seems _____ that Mr. Watson will give the students a test tomorrow.

7. Stu tried to be a _____ son, but sometimes he neglected his chores.

8. Dylan thought it was _____ to the school spirit that the team win on Saturday.

9. Jamila's view was very _____ and not understood by everyone.

10. The speaker said that love is a _____ feeling.

180 Essential Vocabulary Words for 6th Grade © 2009 by Linda Ward Beech, Scholastic Teaching Resources

Name _____ Date _____

appropriate	consistent	cumulative	dutiful	probable
sparse	subjective	trivial	universal	vital

A. Write a vocabulary word for each underlined word in the sentences.

1. How <u>plausible</u> is Stan's excuse? _____

2. It was <u>essential</u> for the candidate to win over more voters. _____

3. Mom says it's not worth worrying over <u>trifling</u> matters. _____

4. Quincy's response was <u>fitting</u> for the occasion. _____

5. The population is <u>thin</u> in this county. _____

6. Usually the boys are <u>obedient</u>, but today they got in trouble. _____

7. Their view on the issue is <u>personal</u>. _____

8. Yuki's position was <u>steady</u> throughout the discussion. _____

B. Read each question. Choose the best answer.

1. Which one is **universal**? ❏ some ❏ all ❏ none

2. Which one is **cumulative**? ❏ snowfall ❏ snowman ❏ snowplow

Portfolio Page

Imagine you are a community organizer. Write an invitation to a group of citizens to a community planning meeting. Use at least three vocabulary words from this lesson.

Name _____ Date _____

appropriate	consistent	cumulative	dutiful	probable
sparse	subjective	trivial	universal	vital

A. A prefix has been added to each lesson word below. Underline the prefix in each word. Then, write a sentence using the word.

1. improbable _____

2. inconsistent _____

3. inappropriate _____

B. Write the base word for each word below. Then, write a sentence using the base word.

1. dutiful _____

_____

2. universal _____

_____

3. subjective _____

_____

4. trivial _____

_____

C. Read the word meaning in each sentence. Then, write a vocabulary word that comes from each Latin word.

1. The Latin word *spargere* means to "scatter." _____

2. The Latin word *vita* means "life." _____

3. The Latin word *cumulus* means "heap." _____

180 Essential Vocabulary Words for 6th Grade © 2009 by Linda Ward Beech, Scholastic Teaching Resources

ADJECTIVES

Name _____ Date _____

Read the clues. Complete the puzzle using vocabulary words.

1. something that is proper or apt

2. someone who is docile and submissive

3. can mean introspective

4. likely to happen

5. unwavering

6. necessary

7. unimportant

8. affecting everyone

9. growing steadily

10. opposite of dense

1. **A** __ __ __ __ __ __ __ __ __ __

2. **D** __ __ __ __ __ __

3. __ __ __ **J** __ __ __ __ __

4. __ __ __ __ __ __ __ **E**

5. **C** __ __ __ __ __ __ __ __

6. __ __ **T** __ __

7. __ __ **I** __ __ __

8. __ __ __ **V** __ __ __

9. __ __ __ __ __ __ __ __ **E**

10. **S** __ __ __ __ __

180 Essential Vocabulary Words for 6th Grade © 2009 by Linda Ward Beech, Scholastic Teaching Resources

NOUNS

Name _____ Date _____

access	apprentice	circumstance	descent	domain
encounter	intelligence	intention	prospect	standard

✱ A NOUN IS A WORD THAT NAMES A PERSON, PLACE, THING, OR CONCEPT. THESE NOUNS ARE USEFUL TO KNOW IN SCHOOL.

If you have **access** to something, you have a means of approaching it.

An **apprentice** works with a mentor to learn a trade or an art.

A **circumstance** is a condition.

Descent is a way down.

A **domain** is an area of control.

An **encounter** is a meeting, usually unexpected.

The ability to acquire and use knowledge is **intelligence**.

An **intention** is a plan.

A **prospect** is a possibility.

A **standard** is an ideal.

Use what you know. Write the best vocabulary word to complete each sentence.

1. The _____ was steep so Hans was careful.

2. Sharon worked as an _____ for a master glassblower.

3. Dad has high _____ , but we try to live up to them.

4. The queen looked out over her _____ and smiled.

5. After their first _____ on the street, the two men always nodded to each other.

6. Do you have _____ to a good library?

7. The students looked for _____ to whom they could sell their raffle tickets.

8. It was Blythe's _____ to dry the dishes, but she forgot.

9. Under no _____ would the boys swim without a lifeguard.

10. Meg's dog can do tricks, but how much _____ does he really have?

100 Essential Vocabulary Words for 6th Grade © 2000 by Linda Ward Beech, Scholastic Teaching Resources

NOUNS

Name _____ Date _____

| access | apprentice | circumstance | descent | domain |
| encounter | intelligence | intention | prospect | standard |

A. In each sentence, circle the vocabulary word and its synonym.

1. Wally discussed his intentions, objectives, and feelings about the project.

2. Each morning the students and apprentices meet with their teachers.

3. Their domain was a far greater realm than we realized.

4. This model will set a standard for years to come.

5. Each circumstance and factor must be considered before we make a decision.

6. The area's descent into crime followed a decline in jobs.

7. Their last meeting was an amazing encounter.

8. Sure that her prospects were good, Gail went to work with expectations of success.

B. Read each question. Choose the best answer.

1. Which one is an **access**? ❒ entrance ❒ closet ❒ exit

2. Which shows **intelligence**? ❒ sinking ❒ blinking ❒ thinking

Portfolio Page

Write a story about an unusual encounter between two characters in a story.
Use at least three vocabulary words from this lesson.

NOUNS

Name _____ Date _____

access	apprentice	circumstance	descent	domain
encounter	intelligence	intention	prospect	standard

A. Some words have more than one meaning. Choose the word that gives the best meaning for the vocabulary word as it's used in each sentence.

1. Omar's **domain** is medieval art. ❒ home ❒ picture ❒ field

2. They acted on **intelligence** from an agent. ❒ information ❒ command ❒ gifts

3. The forty-niners **prospected** for gold. ❒ called ❒ explored ❒ begged

4. Sunil carried the **standard** in the parade. ❒ ideal ❒ banner ❒ stamps

5. Mrs. Marquez **encounters** many problems at her job. ❒ introduces ❒ examines ❒ faces

B. Write an antonym for each word below. Use a dictionary if needed.

1. descent _____   2. apprentice _____

C. Write the number of syllables in each vocabulary word. Then, write the syllables in that word.

Vocabulary Word	Number of Syllables	Syllables
1. access	_____	_____
2. circumstance	_____	_____
3. intention	_____	_____

Name _____ Date _____

Read the clues. Identify the correct vocabulary word and write it next to its clue. Then, find and circle each word in the puzzle.

B	E	L	O	U	A	A	G	M	P	K	N	I
D	I	F	T	Q	I	C	X	W	B	U	S	N
E	P	G	N	E	V	C	J	S	L	O	I	T
S	W	N	D	T	G	E	C	T	Q	E	V	E
C	I	R	C	U	M	S	T	A	N	C	E	L
E	R	H	Y	J	V	S	D	N	B	E	N	L
N	Y	W	M	L	T	J	H	D	L	Z	C	I
T	J	C	Q	P	D	O	M	A	I	N	O	G
P	R	O	S	P	E	C	T	R	S	H	U	E
K	Z	A	M	I	X	F	U	D	O	D	N	N
D	Q	I	N	T	E	N	T	I	O	N	T	C
M	B	Y	H	A	S	Z	R	M	C	X	E	E
F	A	P	P	R	E	N	T	I	C	E	R	W

Hint: The words can run ACROSS or DOWN.

Clues

1. downward movement   _____

2. aim or goal   _____

3. quality   _____

4. learner   _____

5. the means to enter   _____

6. a condition   _____

7. a territory under rule   _____

8. a chance meeting   _____

9. a possibility   _____

10. good thinking   _____

access, p. 74
accomplish, p. 6
adequate, p. 26
aggressive, p. 62
ample, p. 26
annotate, p. 10
anticipate, p. 46
application, p. 6
apprentice, p. 74
approach, p. 42
appropriate, p. 70
articulate, p. 18
assert, p. 18
assume, p. 18
attain, p. 42
attribute, p. 66

benefit, p. 58

calculation, p. 22
capacity, p. 22
capitalism, p. 22
characteristic, p. 10
chronology, p. 54
circumstance, p. 74
clause, p. 14
commit, p. 58
competitive, p. 62
complex, p. 50
component, p. 50
conceive, p. 14
concept, p. 50
confine, p. 66
confront, p. 62
consequence, p. 42
considerate, p. 58
consistent, p. 70
construct, p. 66
consult, p. 6
contend, p. 62
contradict, p. 18
contribution, p. 58
controversy, p. 34
convention, p. 30
converse, p. 18
convey, p. 66
cooperation, p. 58
coordinate, p. 66
credible, p. 46
criteria, p. 50

critique, p. 14
crucial, p. 46
cumulative, p. 70

deny, p. 66
derive, p. 10
descent, p. 74
devise, p. 66
differentiate, p. 42
diminish, p. 26
disclose, p. 18
discriminate, p. 58
displace, p. 38
dispute, p. 30
distinguish, p. 46
distort, p. 34
distribution, p. 22
domain, p. 74
domestic, p. 30
dominate, p. 62
dutiful, p. 70
dynasty, p. 34

effective, p. 14
eliminate, p. 62
emancipate, p. 66
encounter, p. 74
enhance, p. 50
enrich, p. 6
ensure, p. 46
equivalent, p. 26
estate, p. 34
ethics, p. 30
exaggerate, p. 62
exceed, p. 62
exercise, p. 6
extensive, p. 26

financial, p. 22
former, p. 54
formulate, p. 38
foundation, p. 6
fragment, p. 26
frequent, p. 54

generate, p. 50

hereditary, p. 38
hypothesize, p. 38

impact, p. 50

imply, p. 18
informed, p. 58
initial, p. 54
innovation, p. 50
inquiry, p. 38
instantaneous, p. 54
institution, p. 6
intelligence, p. 74
intention, p. 74
interact, p. 6
interpretation, p. 46
intervene, p. 18
irony, p. 10
isolate, p. 66

justify, p. 30

liberate, p. 34
license, p. 30
literal, p. 10
logical, p. 42

magnitude, p. 26
massive, p. 26
maximize, p. 6
media, p. 18
mediate, p. 58
minimal, p. 26
motivation, p. 6

nationalism, p. 34
neutral, p. 34
nuclear, p. 38

obtain, p. 66
ongoing, p. 54
oppose, p. 62
optional, p. 46

panel, p. 30
passive, p. 14
perceive, p. 50
plagiarize, p. 14
plausible, p. 14
potential, p. 46
priority, p. 54
privilege, p. 58
probable, p. 70
produce, p. 22
prompt, p. 54
proportion, p. 22

prospect, p. 74
pursue, p. 62

quorum, p. 26

radical, p. 34
reaction, p. 10
regime, p. 34
reinforce, p. 42
relate, p. 46
relax, p. 46
relevant, p. 42
reside, p. 30
revenue, p. 22
routine, p. 42

scheme, p. 50
significance, p. 10
simultaneous, p. 54
site, p. 30
sparse, p. 70
specify, p. 38
speculate, p. 18
splurge, p. 22
stance, p. 58
standard, p. 74
statistics, p. 22
stress, p. 10
subjective, p. 70
subsequent, p. 54
successor, p. 34
succinct, p. 14
supplement, p. 42
symbolize, p. 10
synthesize, p. 42

theory, p. 38
thesis, p. 14
trajectory, p. 38
transition, p. 14
trivial, p. 70

universal, p. 70

verify, p. 38
version, p. 10
vital, p. 70

welfare, p. 30

LESSON 1

Page 6: 1. maximize 2. consult 3. interact 4. exercise
5. institution 6. accomplish 7. motivation 8. application
9. enrich 10. foundation **Page 7: A.** 1. application 2. consulted
3. foundation 4. interact **B.** 1. synonym—improve; antonym—
diminish 2. synonym—inspiration; antonym—disincentive
3. synonym—achieve; antonym—fail 4. synonym—increase;
antonym—minimize 5. synonym—organization; antonym—
individual 6. synonym—exertion; antonym—inactivity
Page 8: A. 1.–5. Another Related Word: Answers will vary.
1. application 2. interact 3. motivation 4. institution
5. foundation **B.** 1.–5. Sentences will vary.
Page 9: 1. institution 2. exercise 3. accomplish 4. motivation
5. application 6. consult 7. foundation 8. interact 9. maximize
10. enrich

LESSON 2

Page 10: 1. reaction 2. derives 3. significance 4. irony 5. versions
6. characteristic 7. symbolize 8. annotated 9. stress 10. literal
Page 11: A. 1. stress 2. symbolize 3. version 4. derive
5. significance 6. characteristic 7. literal **B.** 1. surprise
2. comment 3. wit **Page 12: A.** 1. iron<u>ical</u> 2. stress<u>ful</u>
3. annotat<u>ion</u> 4. characteristic<u>ally</u> 5. reaction<u>ary</u>. 1.–5. Sentences
will vary. **B.** 1. significance 2. literal 3. derive **C.** 1.–2. Sentences
will vary. **Page 13:** 1. No answer required. 2. stress 3. irony
4. derive 5. version 6. significance 7. characteristic 8. literal
9. annotate 10. reaction

LESSON 3

Page 14: 1. conceive 2. plagiarize 3. succinct 4. clauses
5. transition 6. effective 7. critique 8. thesis 9. plausible
10. passive **Page 15: A.** 1. subtle 2. ridiculous 3. crinkle
4. eventual 5. conclusion 6. conceit 7. recognize **B.** 1. complex
2. essay 3. was eaten **Page 16: A.** 1.–3. Sentences will vary.
1. impassive 2. ineffective 3. implausible **B.** 1. provision
2. dissertation **C.** 1.–5. Sentences will vary. **Page 17:** 1. succinct
2. passive 3. clause 4. critique 5. thesis 6. plagiarize 7. effective
8. conceive 9. plausible 10. transition

LESSON 4

Page 18: 1. converse 2. intervene 3. assume 4. media 5. asserted
6. contradict 7. articulate 8. speculated 9. imply 10. disclose
Page 19: A. 1. claim, insist 2. suggest, hint 3. ponder, reflect
4. uncover, divulge 5. oppose, deny 6. suppose, surmise
7. verbalize, vocalize **B.** 1. mediate 2. magazine 3. telephone
Page 20: A. 1. adopted 2. interfere 3. gambles **B.** 1. disclose
2. contradict 3. articulate **C.** 1.–4. Sentences will vary.
Page 21: 1. articulate 2. disclose 3. intervene 4. converse
5. media 6. assert 7. assume 8. speculate 9. contradict 10. imply;
Riddle answer: conversation

LESSON 5

Page 22: 1. proportion 2. distribution 3. splurged 4. revenue
5. calculation 6. produces 7. statistics 8. capitalism 9. capacity
10. financial **Page 23: A.** 1. manufactured, produced 2. income,
revenues 3. reckoning, calculations 4. distribution, allotment
5. monetary, financial 6. proportion, part **B.** 1. numbers
2. teacup 3. profits 4. extravagant **Page 24: A.** 1.–4. Sentences

will vary. 1. distribute 2. finance 3. capital 4. calculate
B. 1. produce 2. splurge 3. revenue **C.** 1. c 2. b 3. a **Page 25:**
1. calculation 2. capacity 3. statistics 4. financial 5. capitalism
6. produce 7. splurge 8. revenue 9. proportion 10. distribution

LESSON 6

Page 26: 1. massive 2. ample 3. fragment 4. extensive 5. quorum
6. minimal 7. adequate 8. equivalent 9. magnitude
10. diminished **Page 27: A.** 1. synonym—immense; antonym—
scrawny 2. synonym—dwindle; antonym—expand 3. synonym—
appropriate; antonym—insufficient 4. synonym—least;
antonym—maximum 5. synonym—generous; antonym—stingy
6. synonym—widespread; antonym—confined **B.** 1. fragment
2. equivalent 3. magnitude 4. quorum **Page 28: A.** 1. adjective
2. verb 3. adjective 4. noun 5. adjective **B.** 1.–5. Another Related
Word: Answers will vary. 1. extensive 2. minimal 3. magnitude
4. ample 5. fragment **Page 29:** 1. diminish 2. extensive
3. fragment 4. adequate 5. ample 6. quorum 7. equivalent
8. magnitude 9. minimal 10. massive

LESSON 7

Page 30: 1. site 2. ethics 3. license 4. convention 5. reside
6. disputed 7. panel 8. justify 9. welfare 10. domestic **Page 31:**
A. 1. resist 2. contention 3. discourage 4. etiquette 5. sight
6. library 7. jostle 8. welcome **B.** 1. sweeping 2. jury **Page 32:**
A. 1. reside 2. convention 3. dispute 4. ethics 5. justify
B. 1. tame 2. freedom 3. board 4. public relief 5. online page
Page 33: Sample answers: 1. hi 2. side 3. is, put 4. sit, it 5. lice,
ice 6. just, us, if 7. pan, pane, an 8. con, on, vent 9. do, dome,
me, tic 10. we, elf, far, are, fare

LESSON 8

Page 34: 1. dynasty 2. nationalism 3. controversy 4. successor
5. radical 6. distort 7. neutral 8. estate 9. regime 10. liberate
Page 35: A. 1. radical, extreme 2. wrangling, controversy
3. misrepresented, distorted 4. impartial, neutral 5. liberate,
release 6. regime, management 7. nationalism, patriotism
B. 1. next 2. family 3. grand **Page 36: A.** 1. c 2. b 3. b
B. 1. neutral 2. liberate 3. radical **C.** 1.–4. Sentences will vary.
Page 37: 1. neutral 2. liberate 3. radical 4. regime 5. dynasty
6. estate 7. successor 8. controversy 9. distort 10. nationalism

LESSON 9

Page 38: 1. trajectory 2. nuclear 3. displaces 4. hereditary
5. hypothesized 6. specify 7. formulated 8. verify 9. theory
10. inquiry **Page 39: A.** 1. inquiry 2. hereditary 3. displace
4. formulate 5. specify 6. trajectory 7. hypothesized 8. verify
B. 1. hypothesis 2. submarine **Page 40: A.** 1. verb 2. adjective
3. noun 4. verb 5. verb 6. adjective **B.** 1. trajectory
2. hypothesize 3. theory **C.** 1.–2. Sentences will vary. 1. misplace
2. replace **Page 41:** 1. displace 2. inquiry 3. specify 4. verify
5. formulate 6. hereditary 7. hypothesize 8. nuclear 9. theory
10. trajectory

LESSON 10

Page 42: 1. routine 2. reinforce 3. relevant 4. approach 5. attain
6. consequence 7. synthesize 8. differentiate 9. supplement
10. logical **Page 43: A.** 1. attain 2. relevant 3. logical

4. consequence 5. routine 6. differentiate **B.** 1. homework
2. skills 3. chapters 4. appendix **Page 44: A.** 1. routine<u>ly</u>, adverb
2. reinforce<u>ment</u>, noun 3. supplement<u>al</u>, adjective
4. approach<u>able</u>, adjective 5. attain<u>ment</u>, noun **B.** 1.–2.
Sentences will vary. 1. <u>il</u>logical 2. <u>ir</u>relevant **C.** 1.–3. Sentences
will vary. **Page 45:** 1. No answer required. 2. consequence 3.
discriminate 4. attain 5. routine 6. logical 7. supplement 8.
approach
9. reinforce 10. relevant

LESSON 11
Page 46: 1. relax 2. anticipate 3. crucial 4. ensure
5. interpretation 6. distinguish 7. relate 8. potential 9. credible
10. optional **Page 47: A.** 1. potential 2. interpretation 3. credible
4. related 5. distinguish 6. crucial 7. relaxed 8. ensure **B.** 1. the
future 2. elective **Page 48: A.** Sample answers: 1. unbelievable 2.
required 3. unimportant 4. strain 5. blur **B.** 1.–3. Another
Related Word: Answers will vary. 1. interpretation 2. anticipate
3. relate **C.** 1.–2. Sentences will vary. **Page 49:** Riddle answer:
cupcake. Synonym pairs: slacken, relax; secure, ensure;
important, crucial; reliable, credible; optional, elective; expect,
anticipate; distinguish, differentiate; interpretation, clarification;
link, relate; potential, possible

LESSON 12
Page 50: 1. generate 2. complex 3. impact 4. enhance 5. scheme
6. concept 7. perceives 8. innovation 9. criteria 10. component
Page 51: A. 1. perceive 2. complex 3. enhance 4. concept
5. component 6. generate 7. innovation 8. impact **B.** 1. plot
2. rules **Page 52: A.** 1. b 2. b 3. a **B.** 1. fear 2. blow 3. understand
C. 1. 3; com/po/nent 2. 1; scheme 3. 2; con/cept
4. 4; in/no/va/tion **Page 53:** 1. enhance 2. criteria 3. concept
4. innovation 5. scheme 6. generate 7. perceive 8. complex
9. impact 10. component

LESSON 13
Page 54: 1. prompt 2. frequent 3. chronology 4. initial 5. former
6. instantaneous 7. priority 8. subsequent 9. simultaneous
10. ongoing **Page 55: A.** 1. synonym—punctual; antonym—late
2. synonym—beginning; antonym—final 3. synonym—
succeeding; antonym—earlier 4. synonym—repeatedly;
antonym—seldom 5. synonym—immediate; antonym—eventual
6. synonym—perpetual; antonym—limited 7. synonym—
concurrent; antonym—alternate **B.** 1. timeline 2. last year
3. schoolwork **Page 56: A.** 1. adjective 2. noun 3. adjective
4. adjective **B.** 1. initial 2. chronology 3. frequent
4. instantaneous **C.** 1.–2. Sentences will vary. **Page 57:** 1. former
2. prompt 3. chronology 4. ongoing 5. initial 6. frequent
7. instantaneous 8. priority 9. subsequent 10. simultaneous

LESSON 14
Page 58: 1. informed 2. benefit 3. stance 4. privilege 5. mediate
6. contributions 7. considerate 8. cooperation 9. discriminate
10. committed **Page 59: A.** 1. informed, knowledgeable 2. settle,
mediate 3. thoughtful, considerate 4. donation, contribution
5. committed, promised 6. stance, position **B.** 1. unfairness
2. assistance 3. advantage 4. individual **Page 60: A.** 1.–5.

Another Related Word: Answers will vary. 1. benefit
2. contribution 3. discriminate 4. mediate 5. cooperation
B. 1.–3. Sentences will vary. **C.** Sample answers: 1. inconsiderate
2. uninformed **Page 61:** Sample answers: 1. it 2. vile, leg 3. fit, it
4. tan, an 5. me, media, at, ate 6. con, on, rib, but 7. is, rim, in,
at, ate 8. coop, era, rat, at, on 9. in, for, form, or, me 10. con, on,
side, era, rat, rate, at, ate

LESSON 15
Page 62: 1. exceeded 2. eliminate 3. competitive 4. oppose
5. exaggerate 6. dominates 7. pursued 8. confronted 9. contend
10. aggressive **Page 63: A.** 1. surpass, outdo 2. control, govern
3. ardent, zealous 4. boast, magnify 5. remove, discard 6. follow,
chase 7. face, encounter **B.** 1. against 2. racer 3. contestant
Page 64: A. 1. contend<u>er</u>, noun 2. domina<u>tion</u>, noun
3. aggressive<u>ly</u>, adverb 4. competitive<u>ly</u>, adverb **B.** Sample
answers: 1. approve 2. add 3. underachieve **C.** 1. b 2. c 3. b
Page 65: 1. exceed 2. oppose 3. aggressive 4. eliminate 5. pursue
6. contend 7. exaggerate 8. dominate
9. confront 10. competitive

LESSON 16
Page 66: 1. convey 2. obtain 3. isolate 4. coordinate 5. confined
6. deny 7. construct 8. emancipate 9. attributed 10. devise
Page 67: A. 1. confine 2. construct 3. attribute 4. deny 5. devise
6. emancipate 7. convey 8. obtain **B.** 1. fair 2. lighthouse
Page 68: A. 1. quality 2. refuse 3. communicated 4. numbers
B. 1.–4. Another Related Word: Answers will vary. 1. construct
2. emancipate 3. isolate 4. obtain **C.** 1.–2. Sentences will vary.
Page 69: 1. deny 2. confine 3. emancipate 4. isolate 5. devise
6. construct 7. obtain 8. attribute 9. coordinate 10. convey

LESSON 17
Page 70: 1. cumulative 2. sparse 3. appropriate 4. trivial
5. consistent 6. probable 7. dutiful 8. vital 9. subjective
10. universal **Page 71: A.** 1. probable 2. vital 3. trivial
4. appropriate 5. sparse 6. dutiful 7. subjective 8. consistent
B. 1. all 2. snowfall **Page 72: A.** 1.–3. Sentences will vary.
1. <u>im</u>probable 2. <u>in</u>consistent 3. <u>in</u>appropriate **B.** 1.–4. Sentences
will vary. 1. duty 2. universe 3. subject 4. trivia. **C.** 1. sparse
2. vital 3. cumulative **Page 73:** 1. appropriate 2. dutiful
3. subjective 4. probable 5. consistent 6. vital 7. trivial
8. universal 9. cumulative 10. sparse

LESSON 18
Page 74: 1. descent 2. apprentice 3. standards 4. domain
5. encounter 6. access 7. prospects 8. intention 9. circumstance
10. intelligence **Page 75: A.** 1. intentions, objectives 2. students,
apprentices 3. domain, realm 4. model, standard
5. circumstance, factor 6. descent, decline 7. meeting, encounter
8. prospects, expectations **B.** 1. entrance 2. thinking
Page 76: A. 1. field 2. information 3. explored 4. banner 5. faces
B. Sample answers: 1. ascent 2. teacher **C.** 1. 2, ac/cess 2. 3,
cir/cum/stance 3. 3, in/ten/tion **Page 77:** 1. descent 2. intention
3. standard 4. apprentice 5. access 6. circumstance 7. domain 8.
encounter 9. prospect 10. intelligence